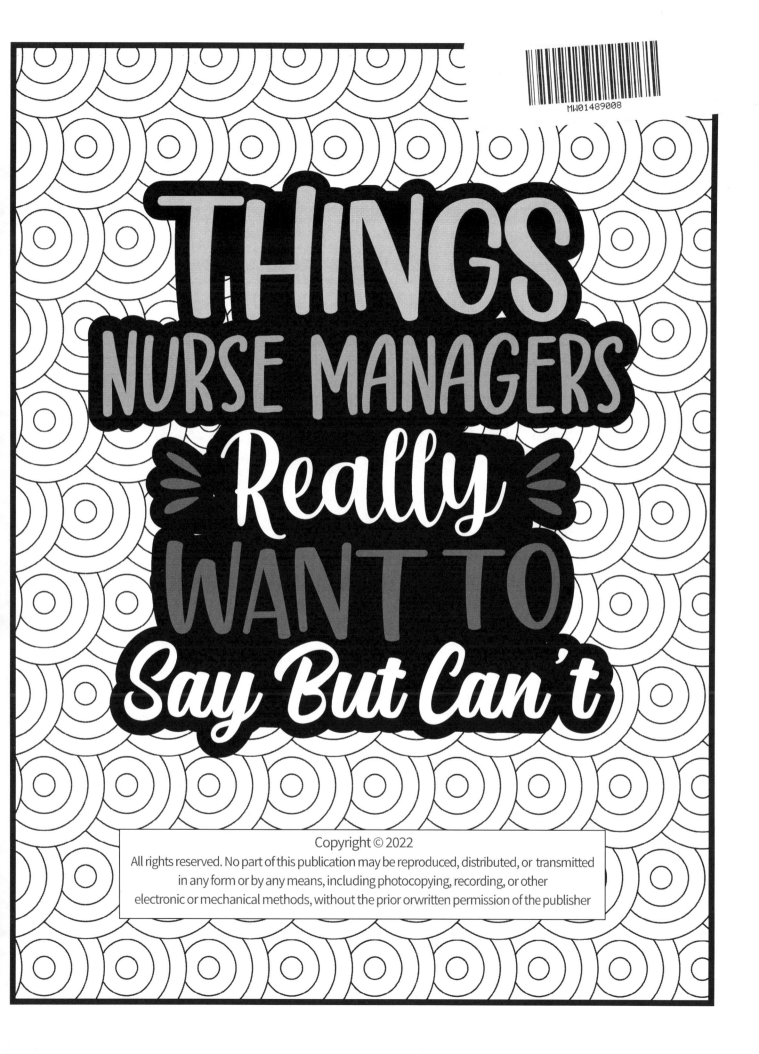

THINGS NURSE MANAGERS Really WANT TO Say But Can't

MW01489008

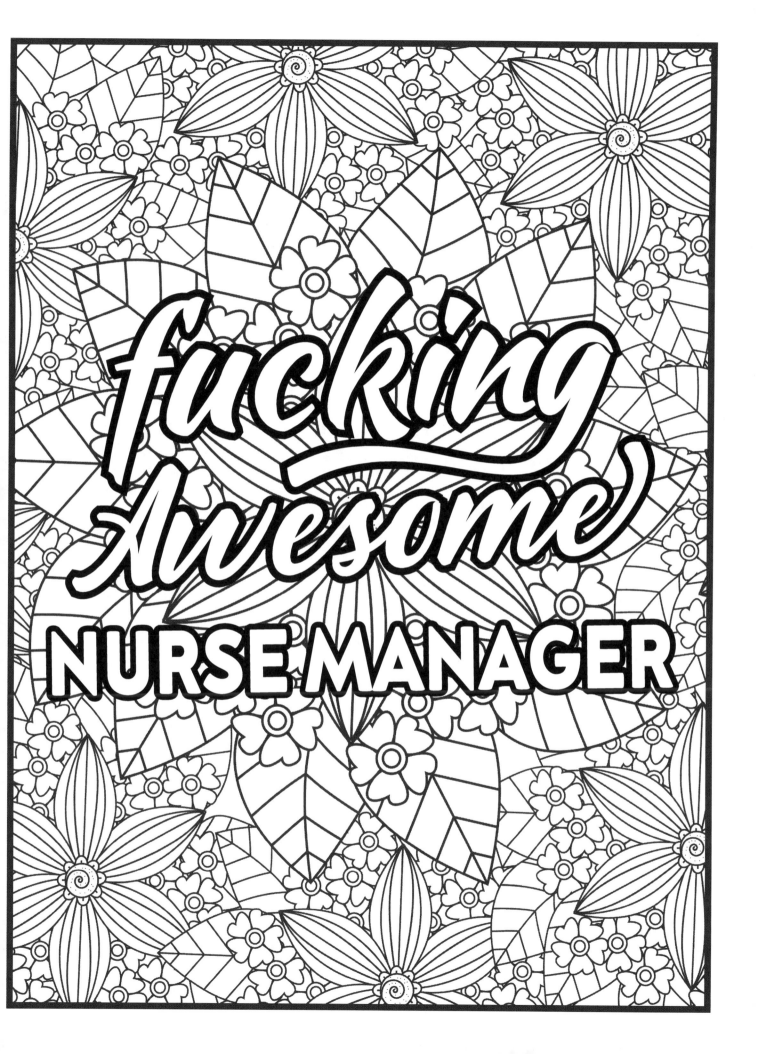

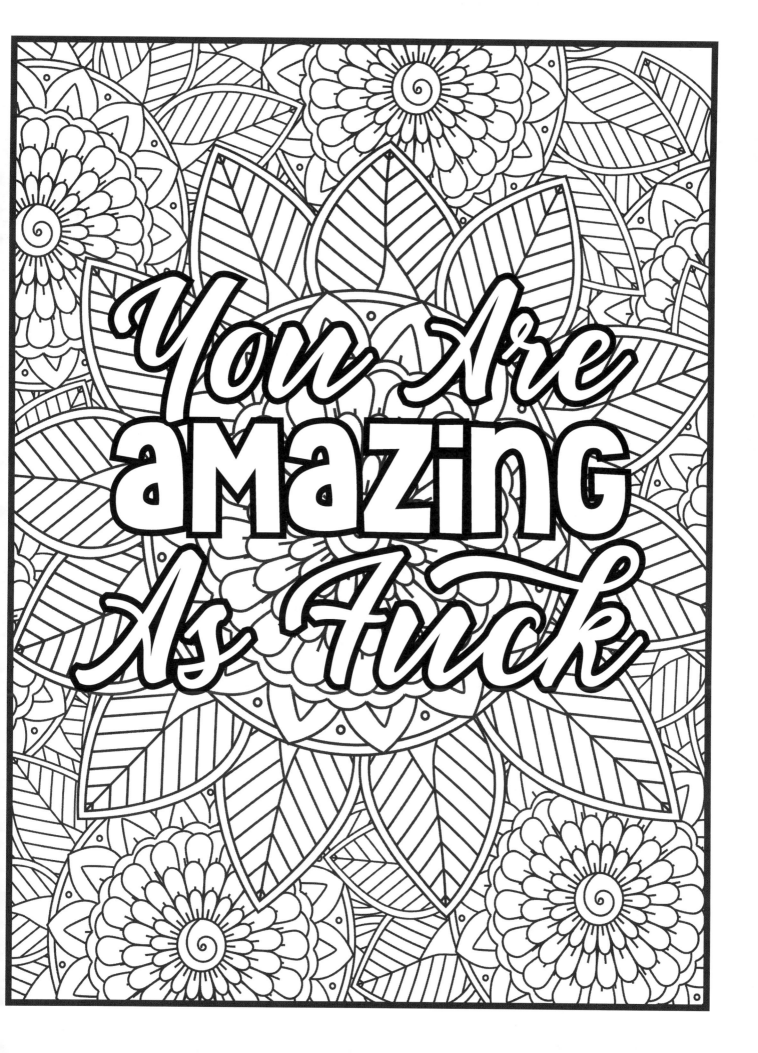

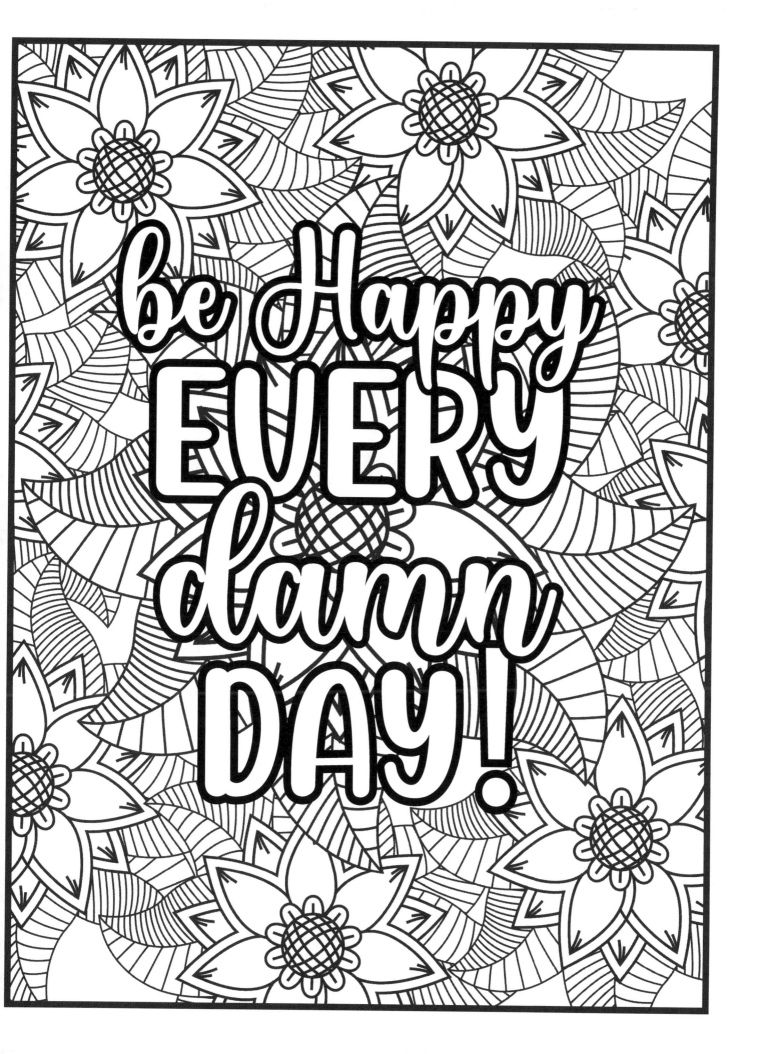

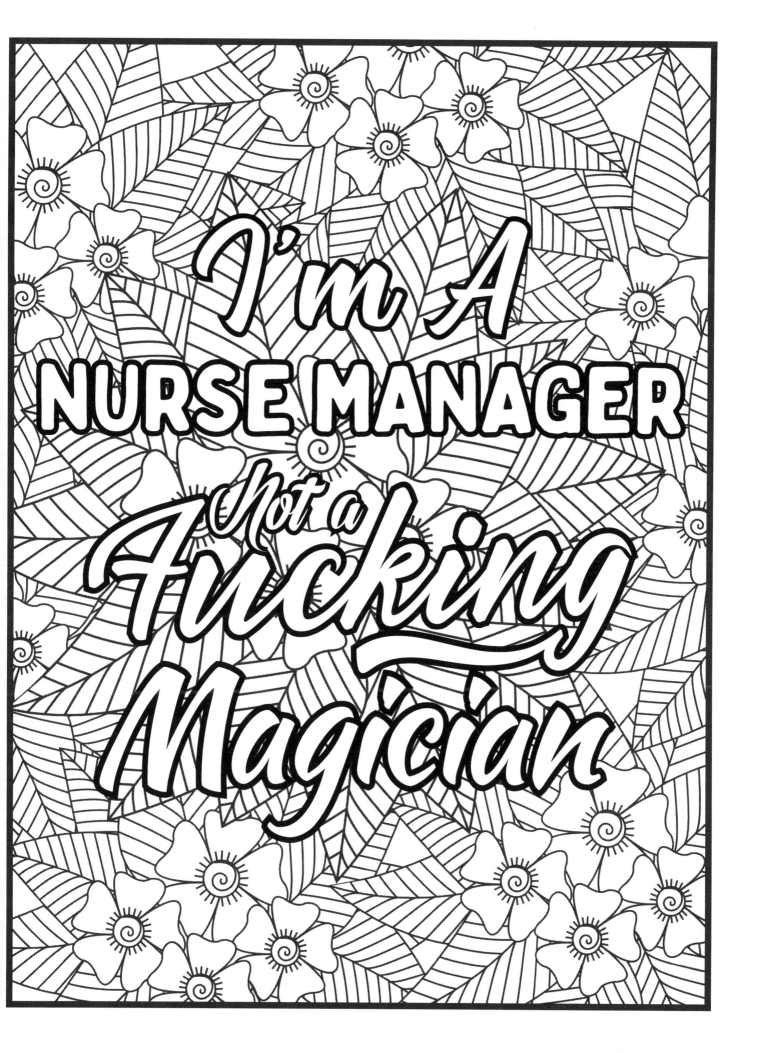

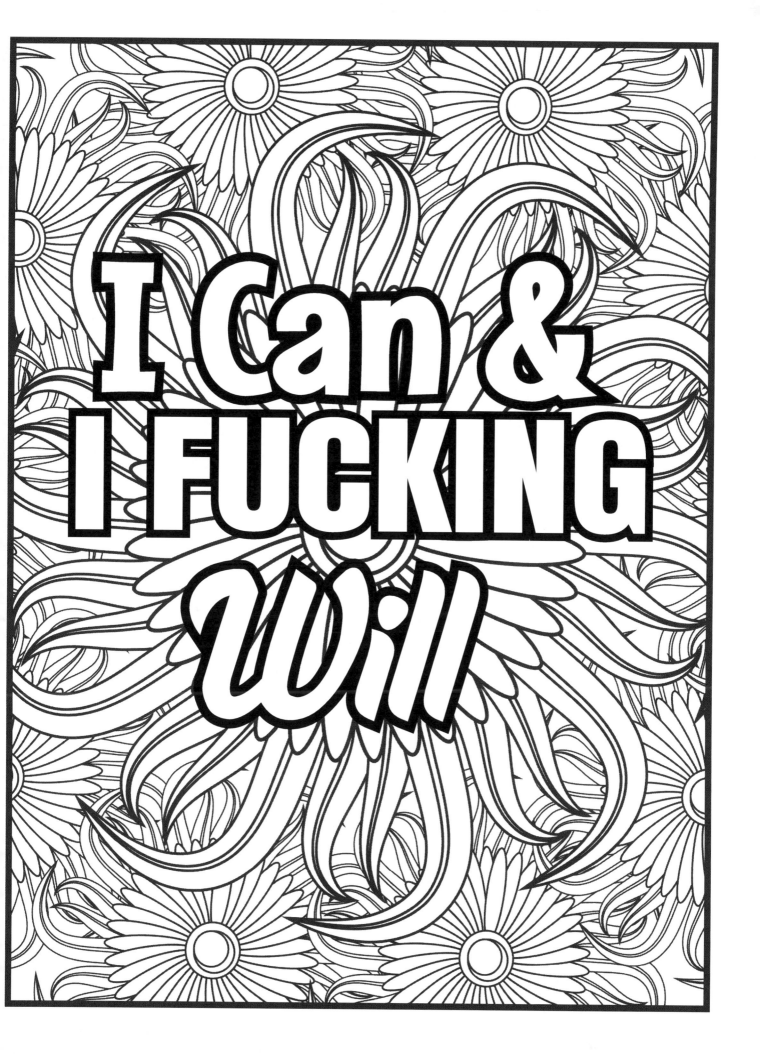

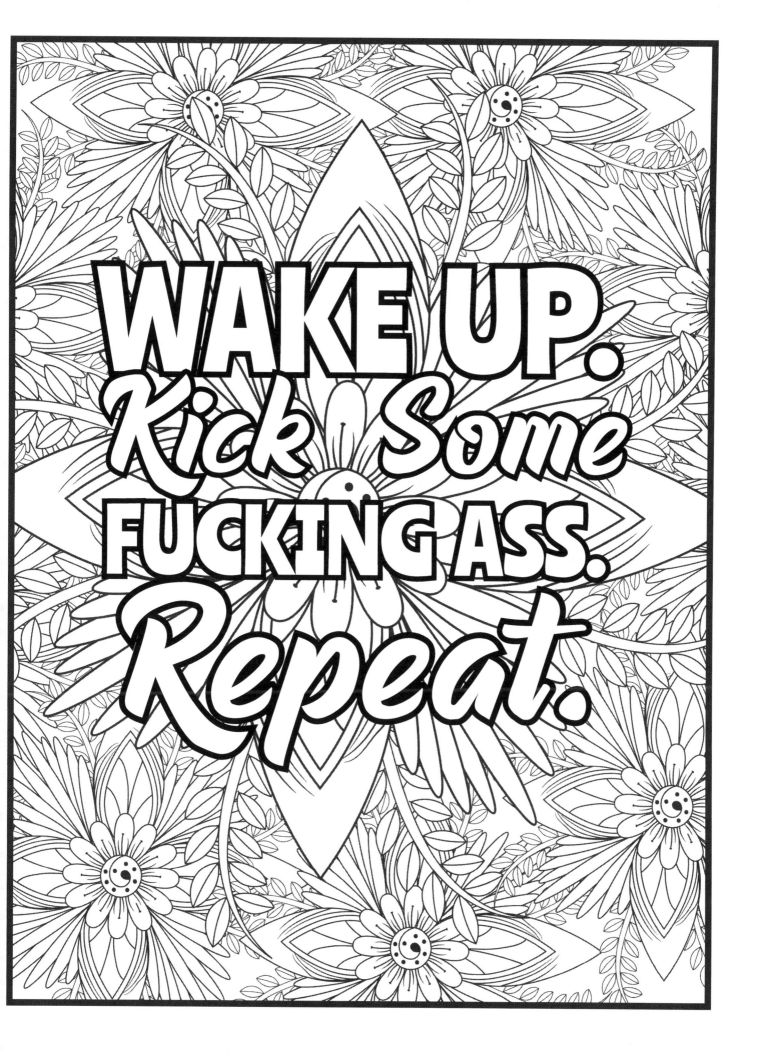

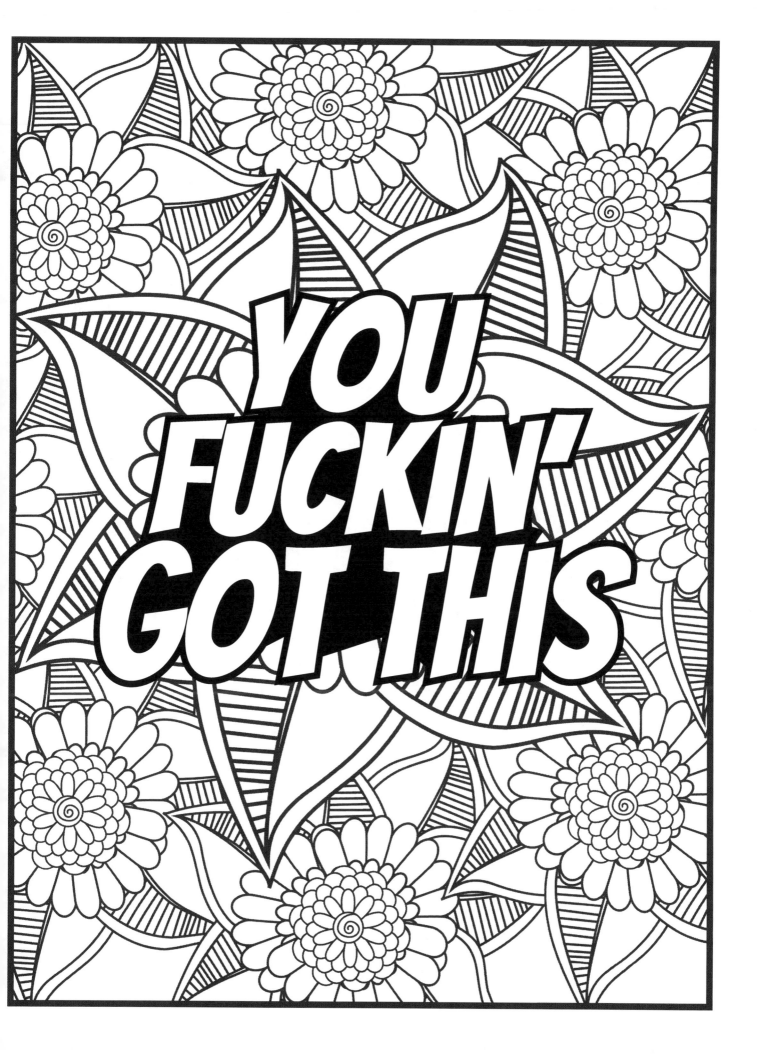

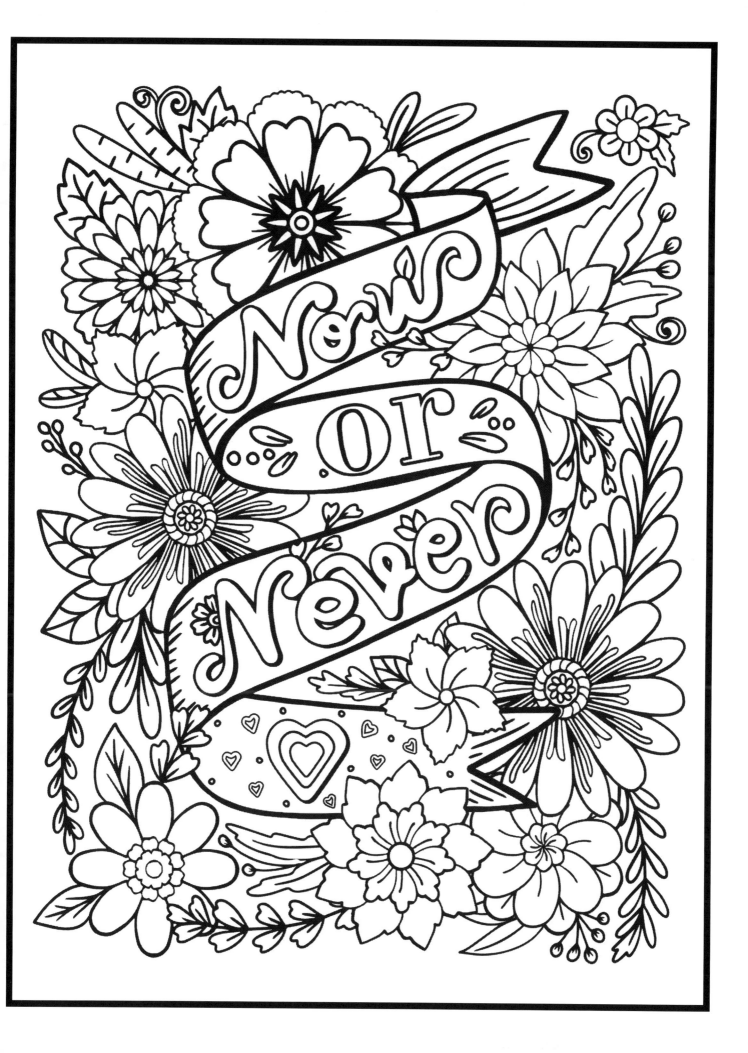

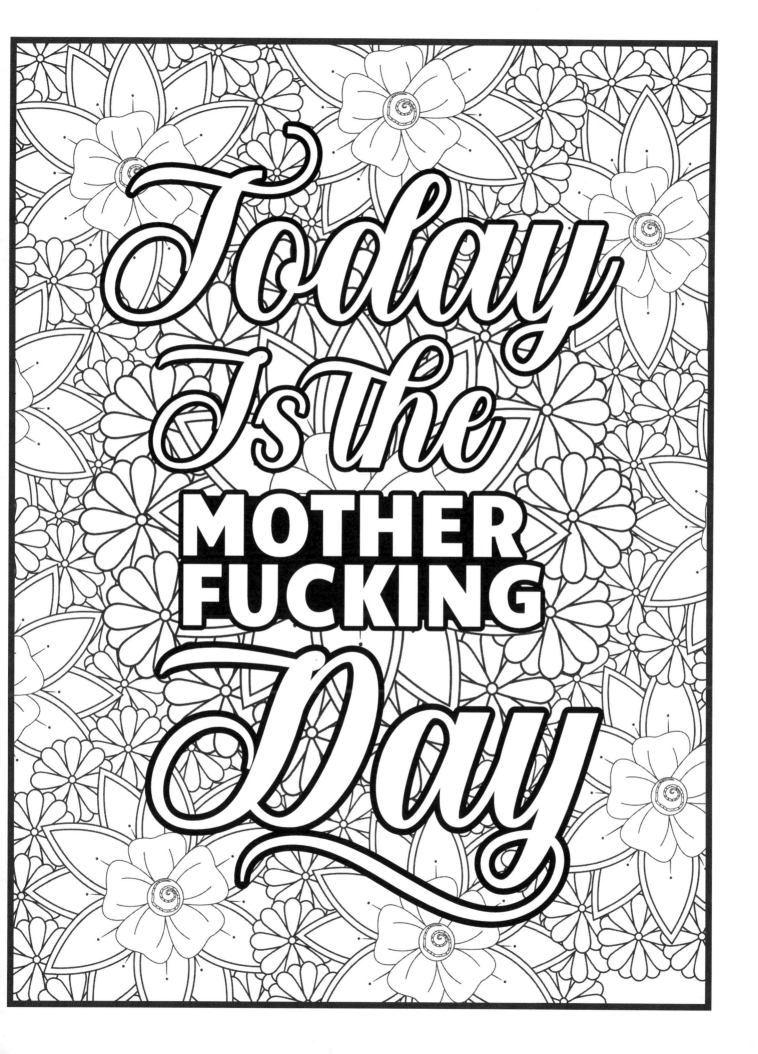

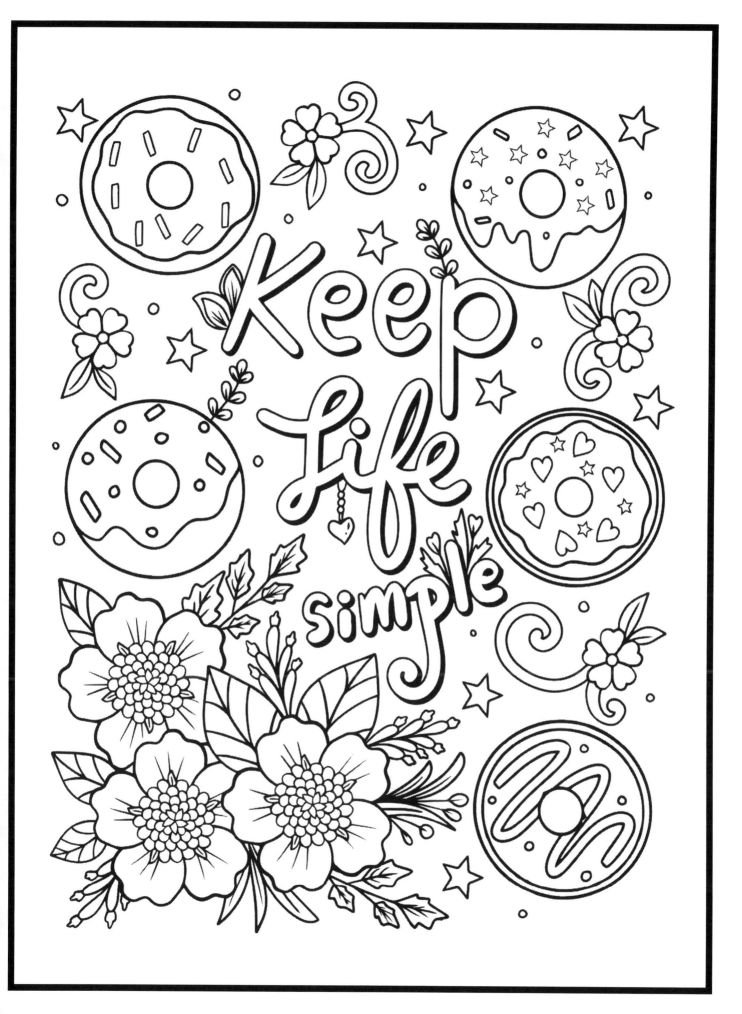

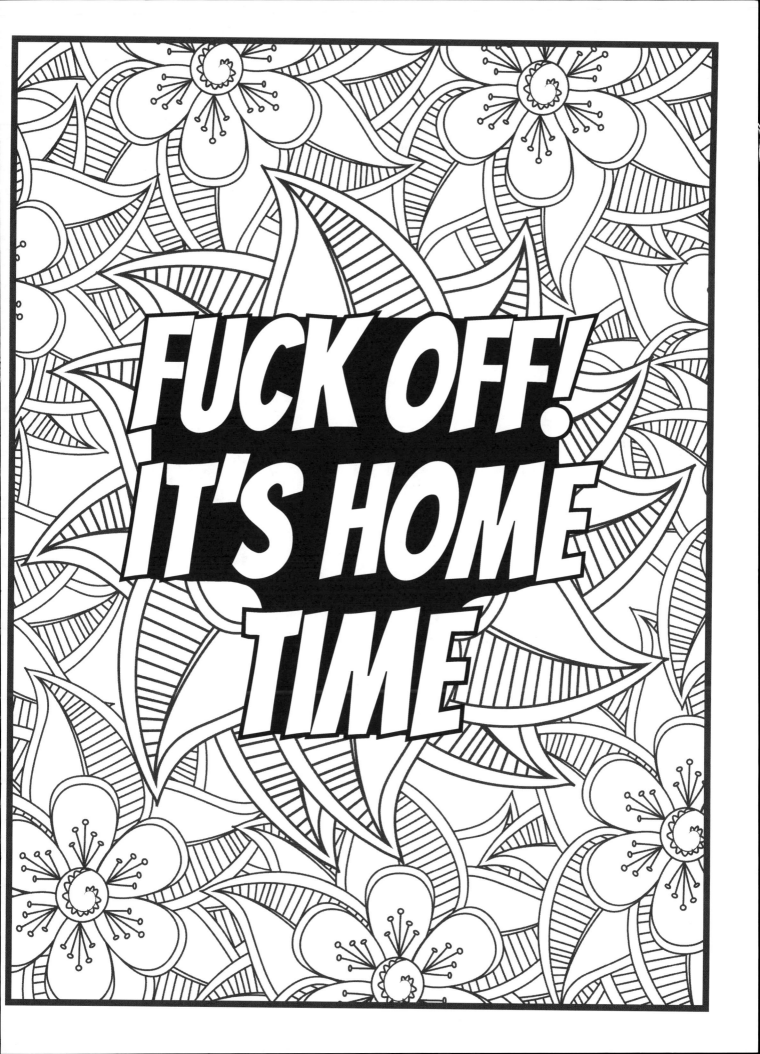

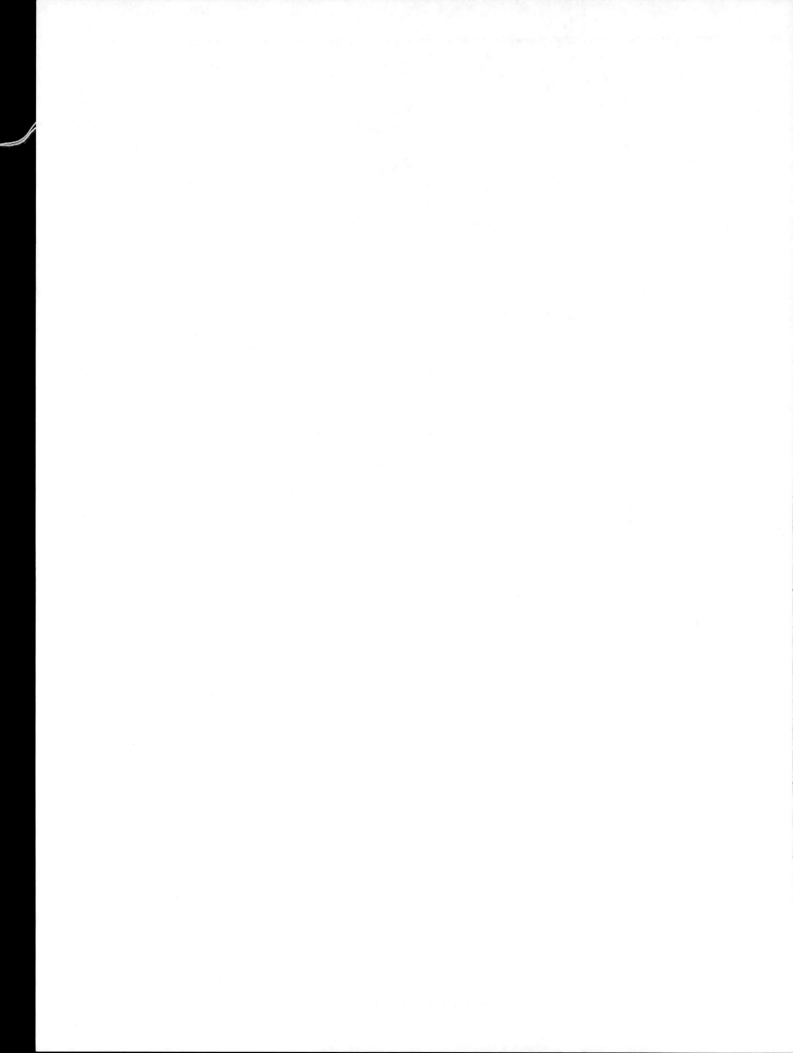

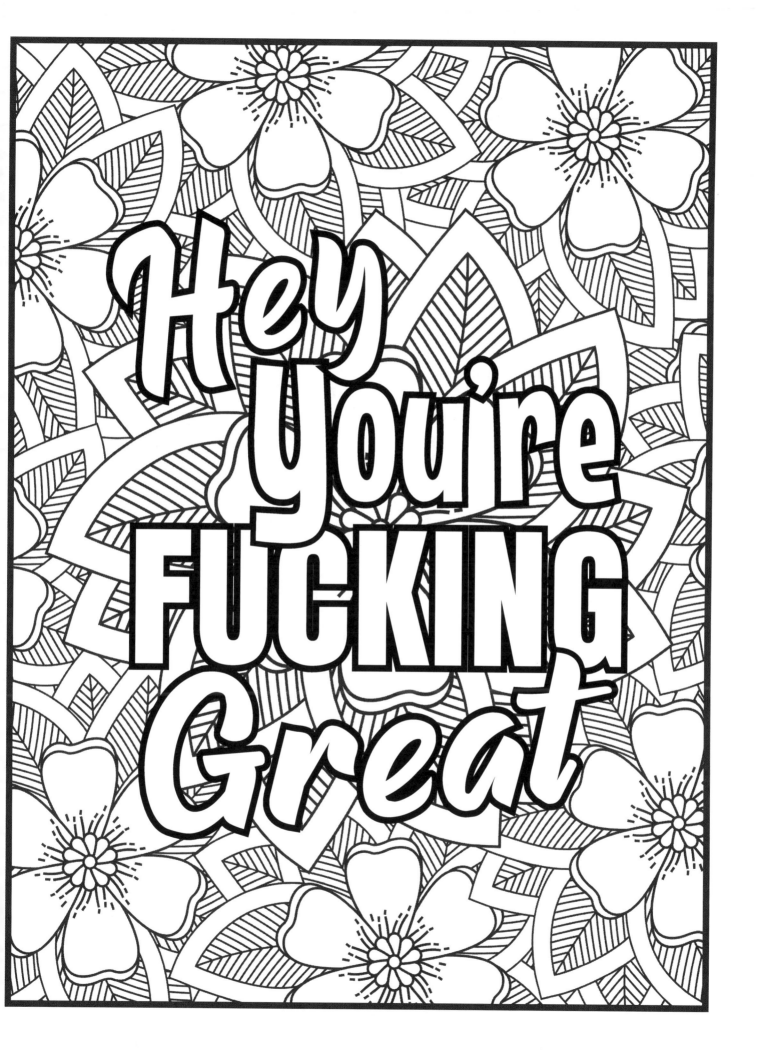

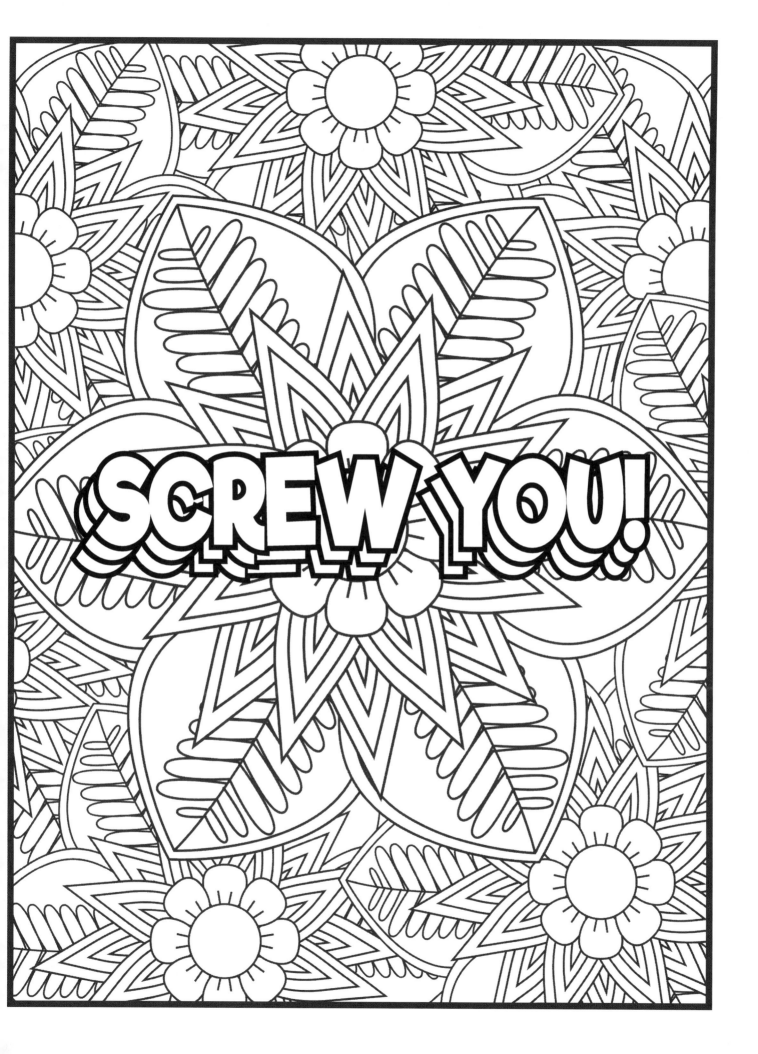

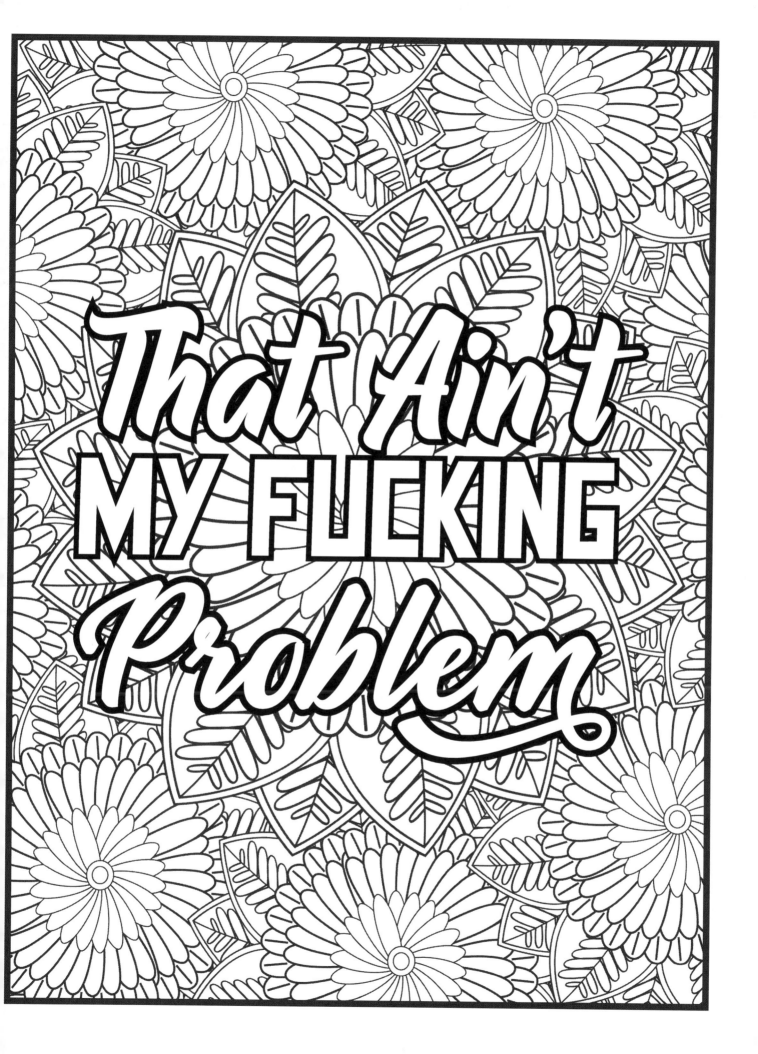

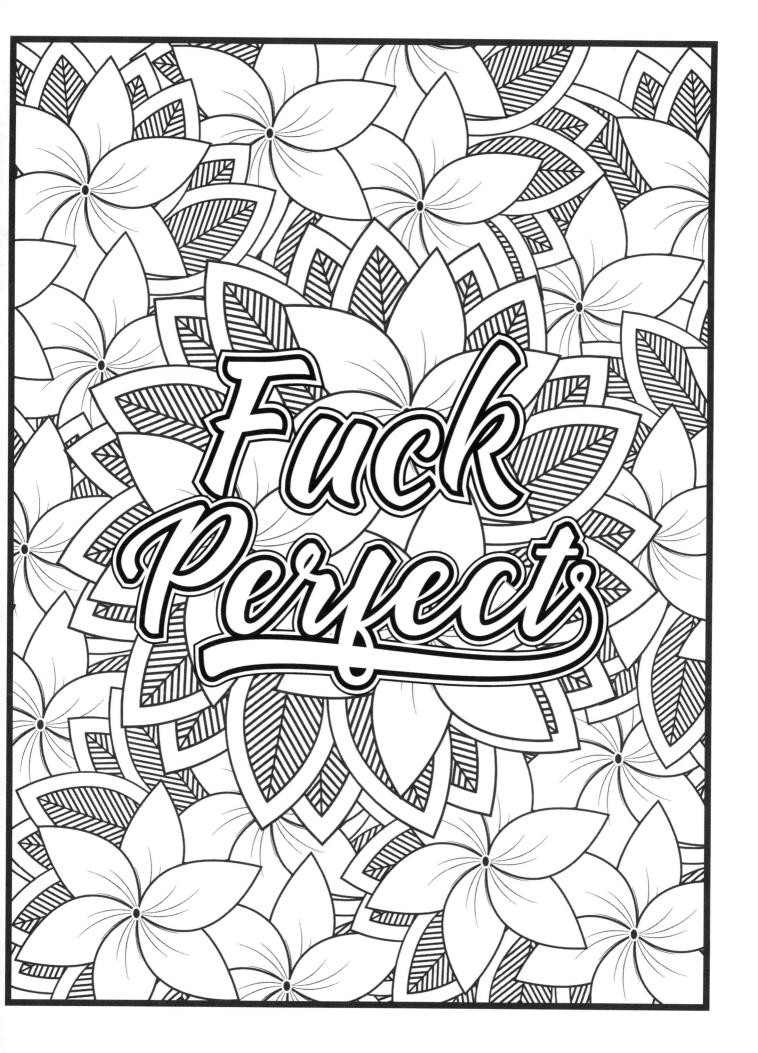

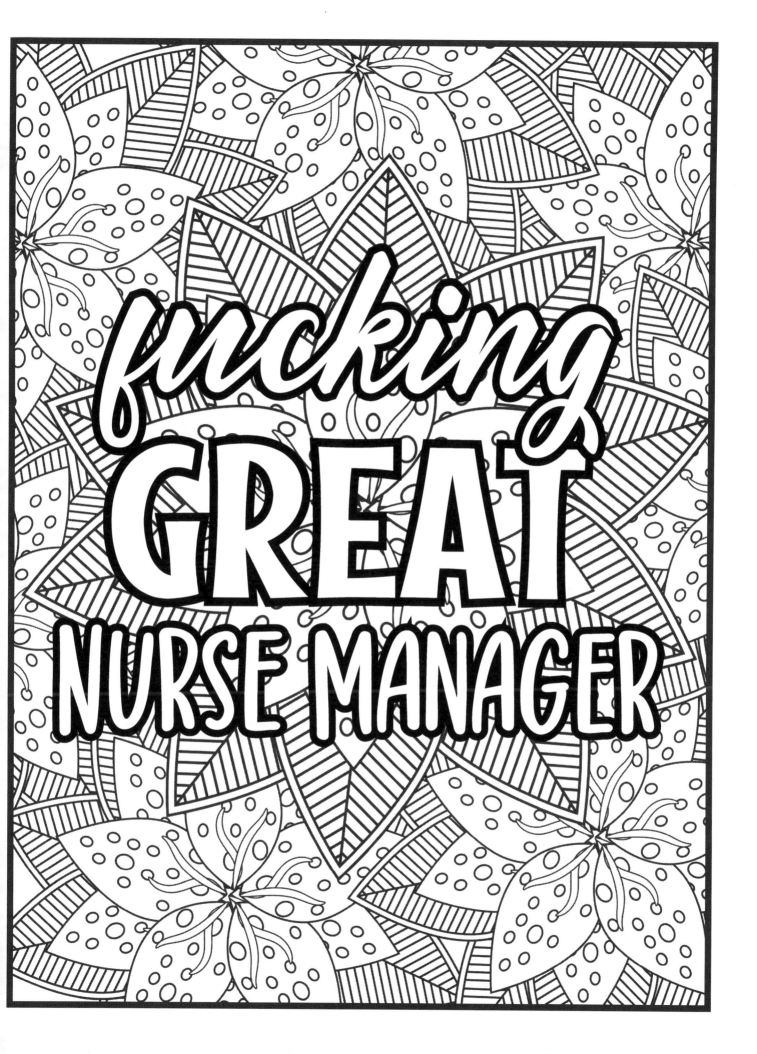

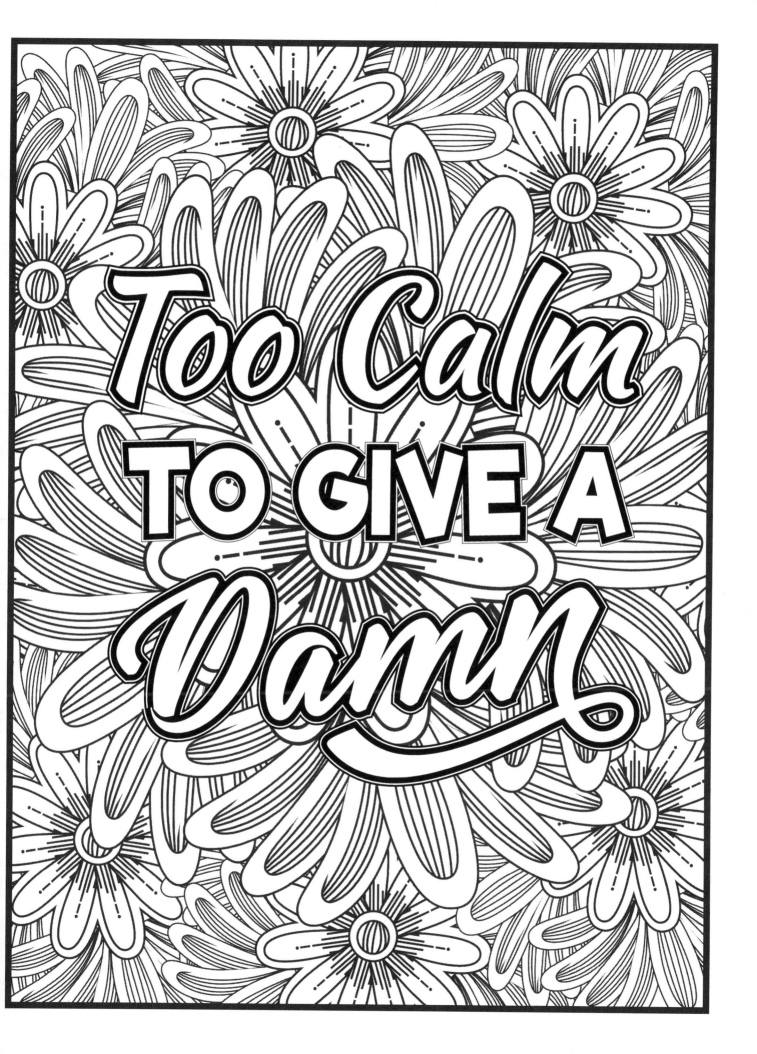

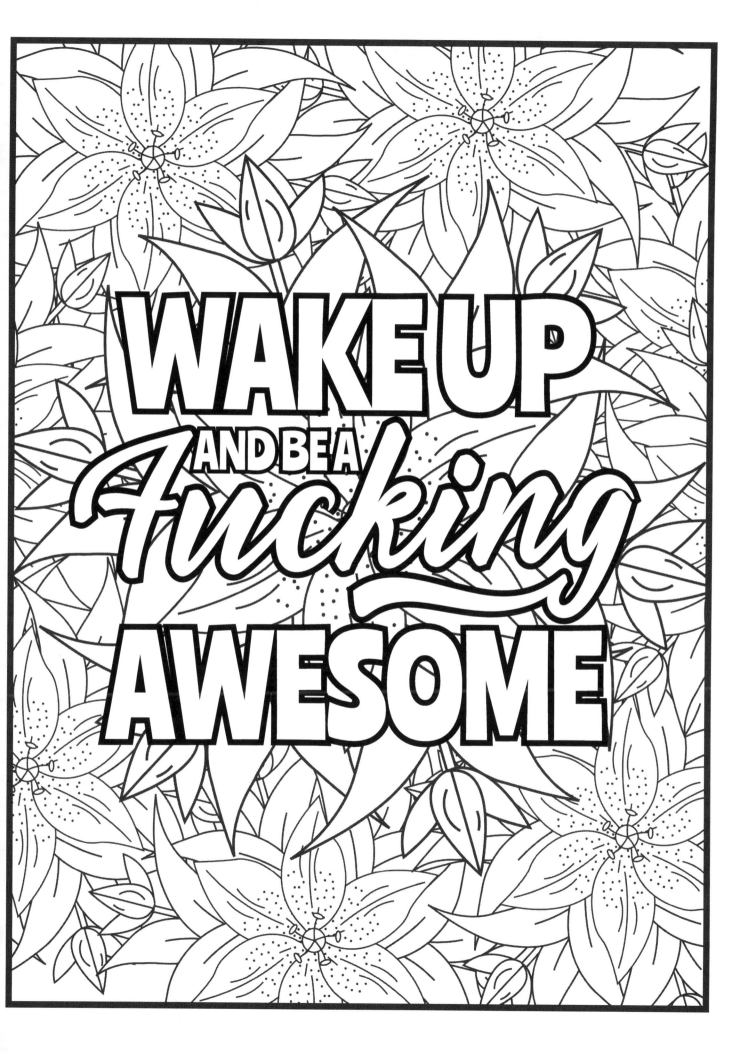

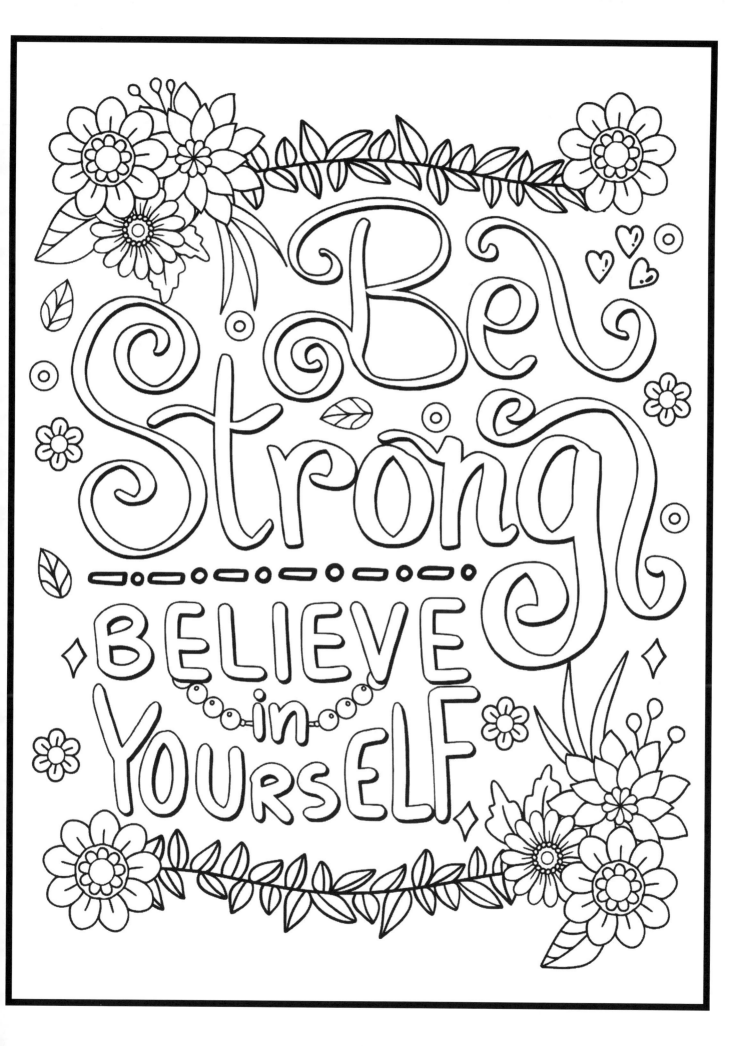

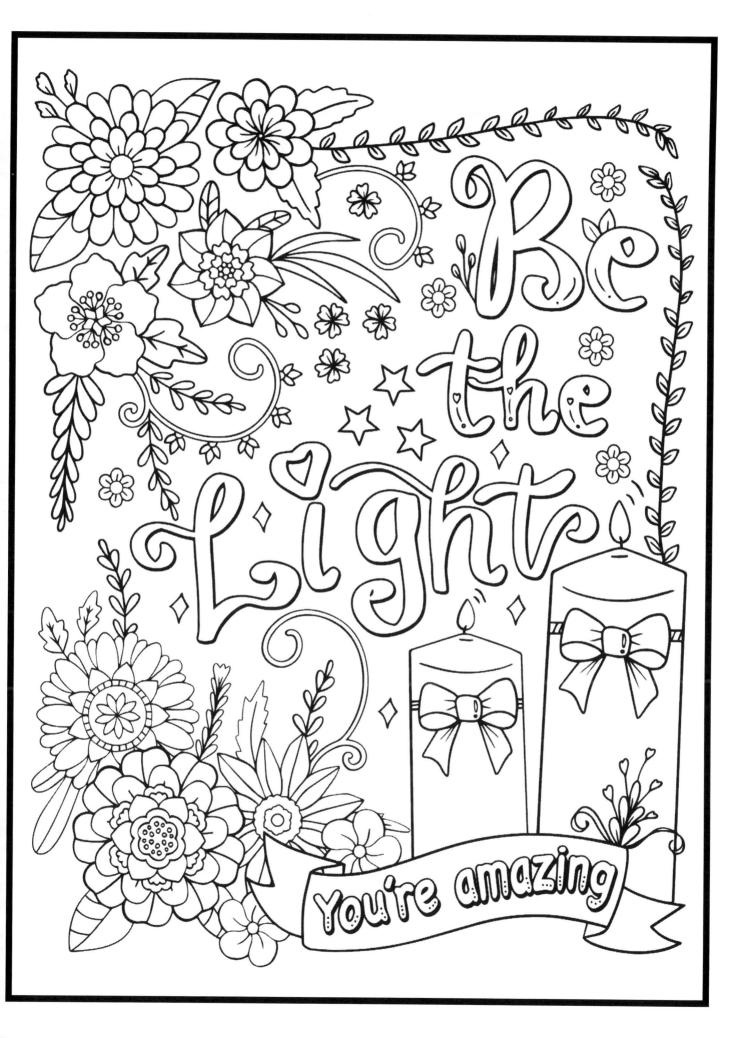

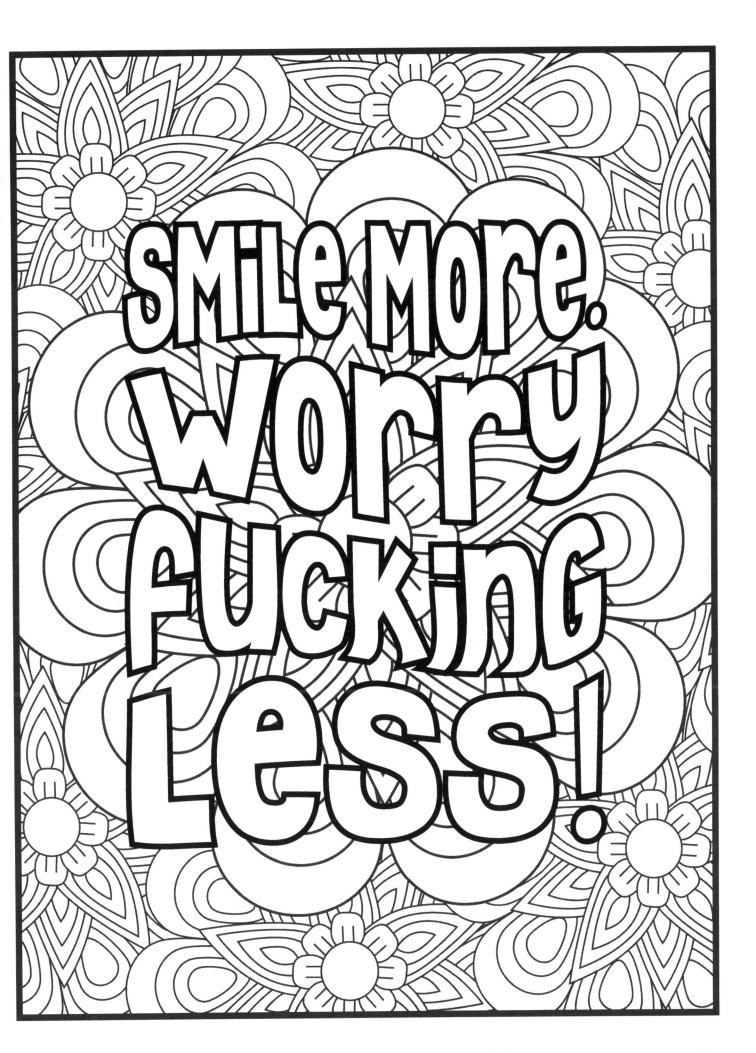

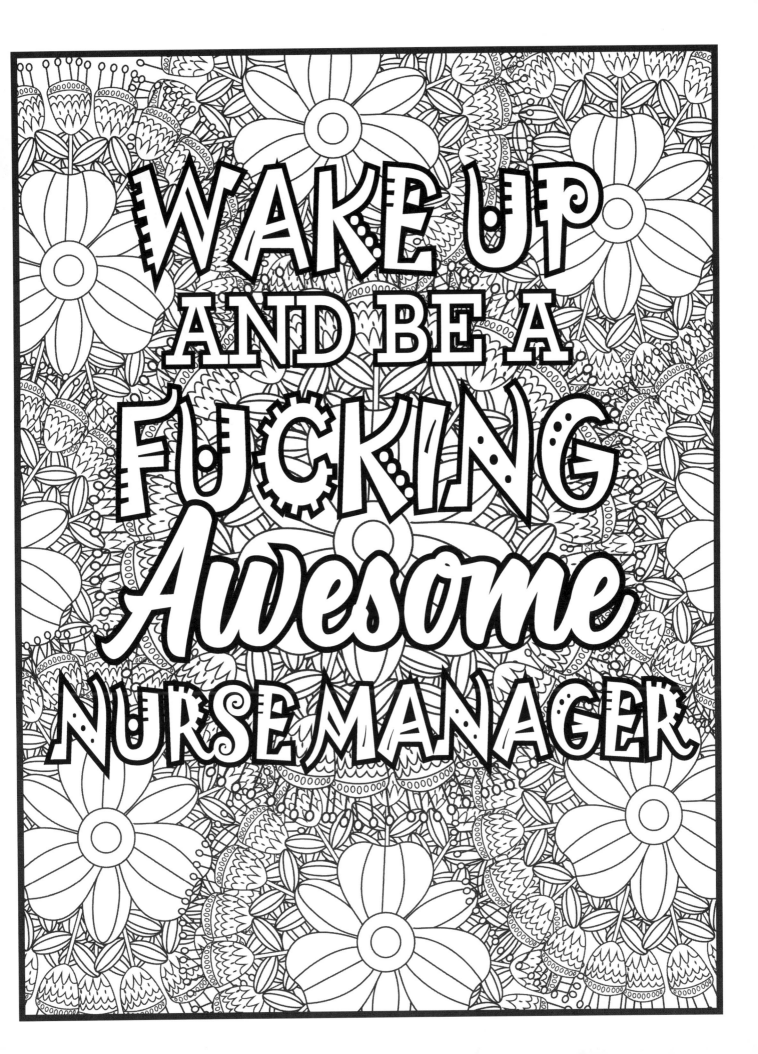

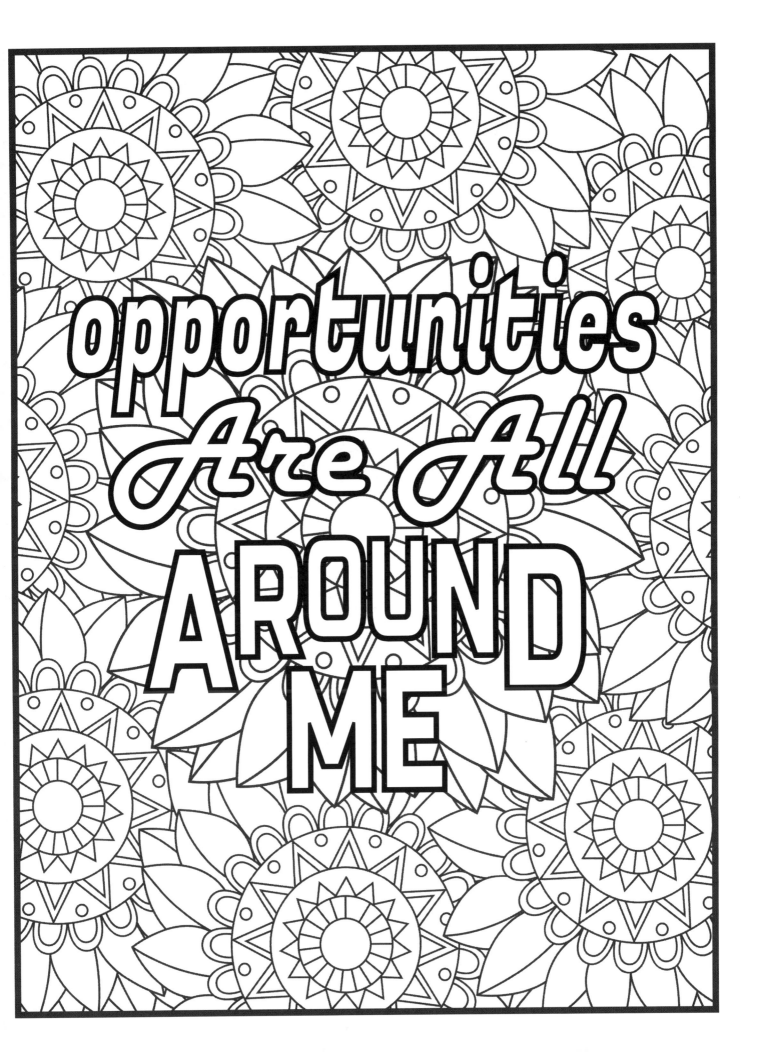

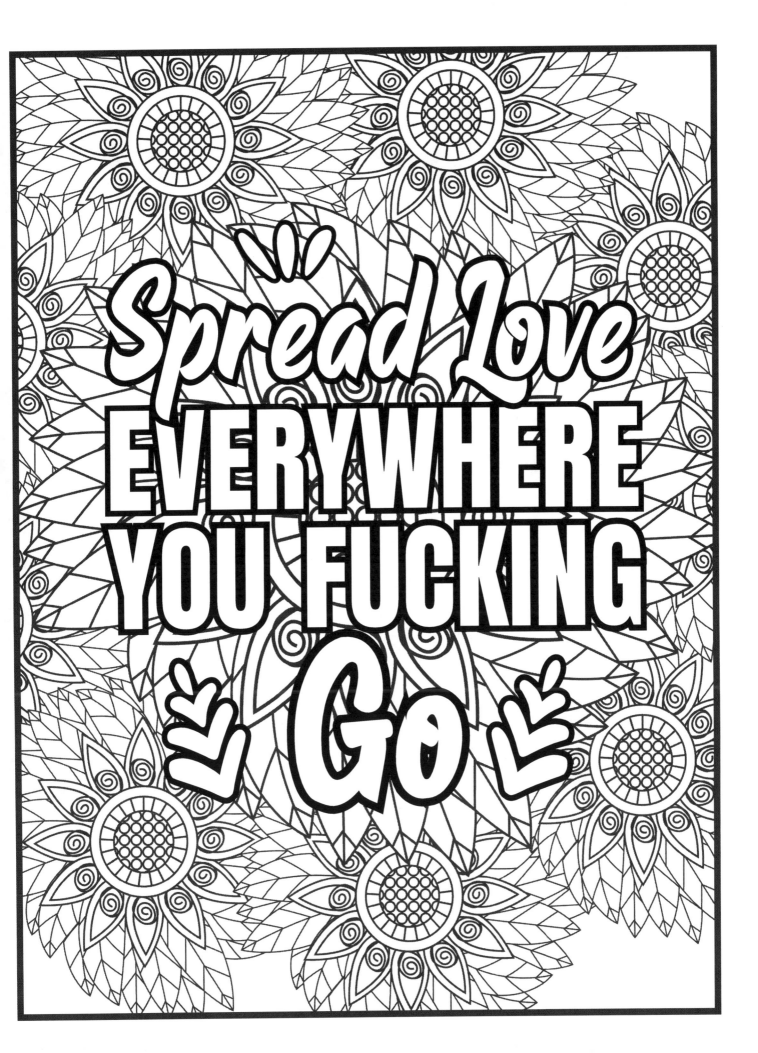

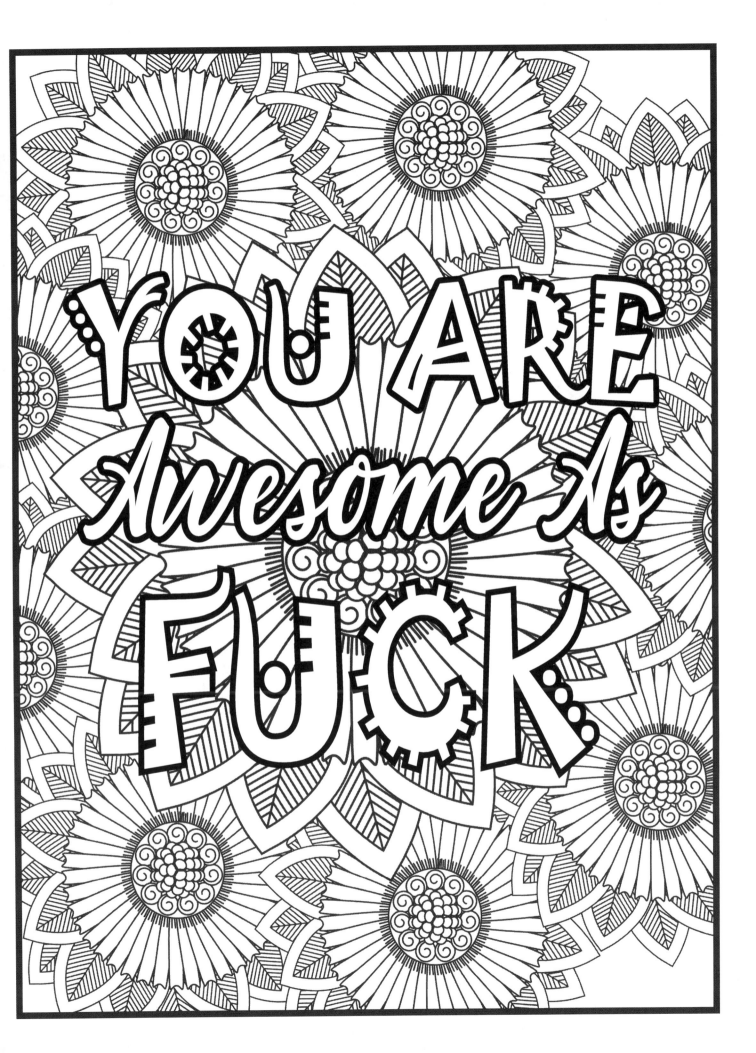

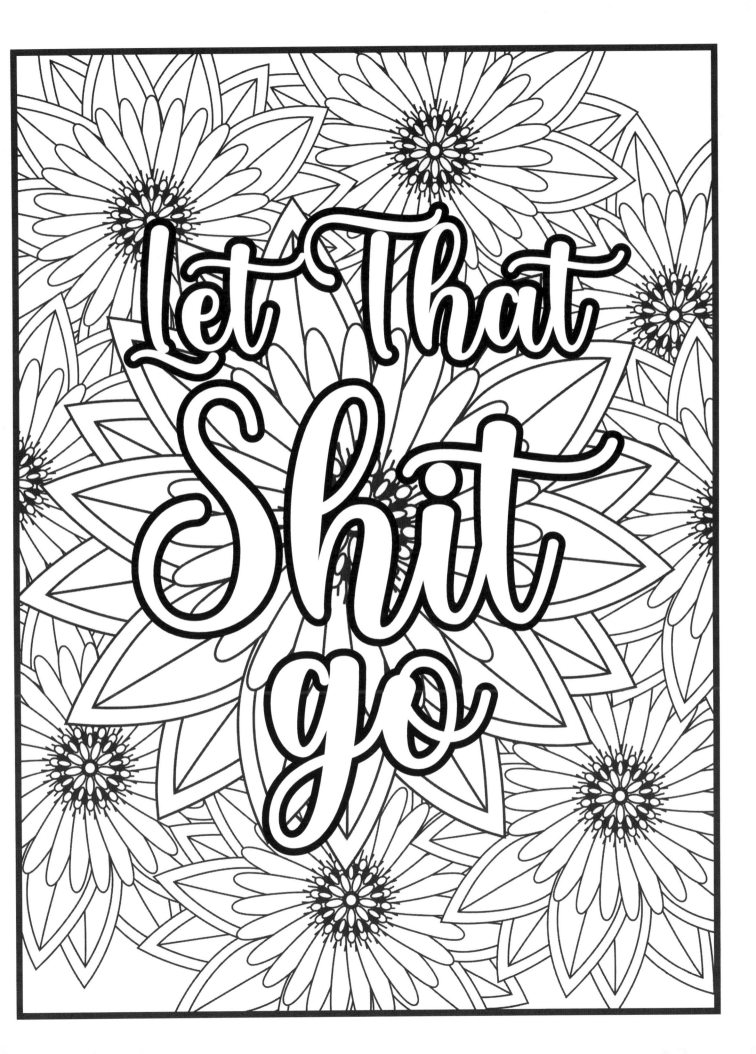

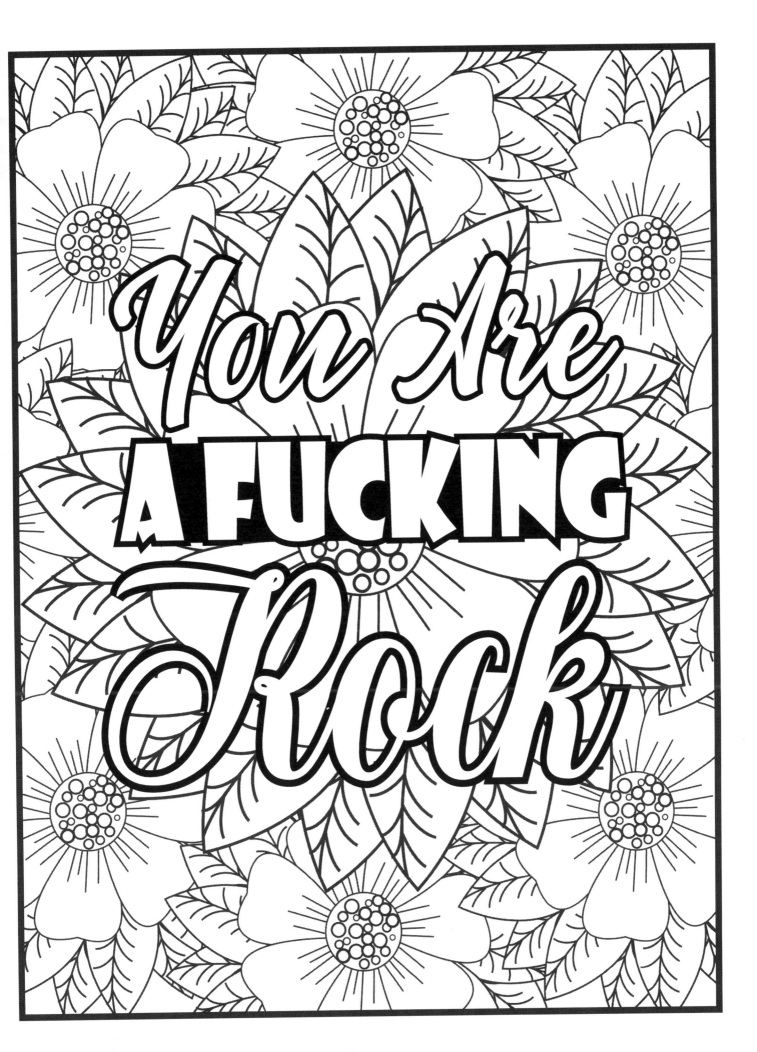

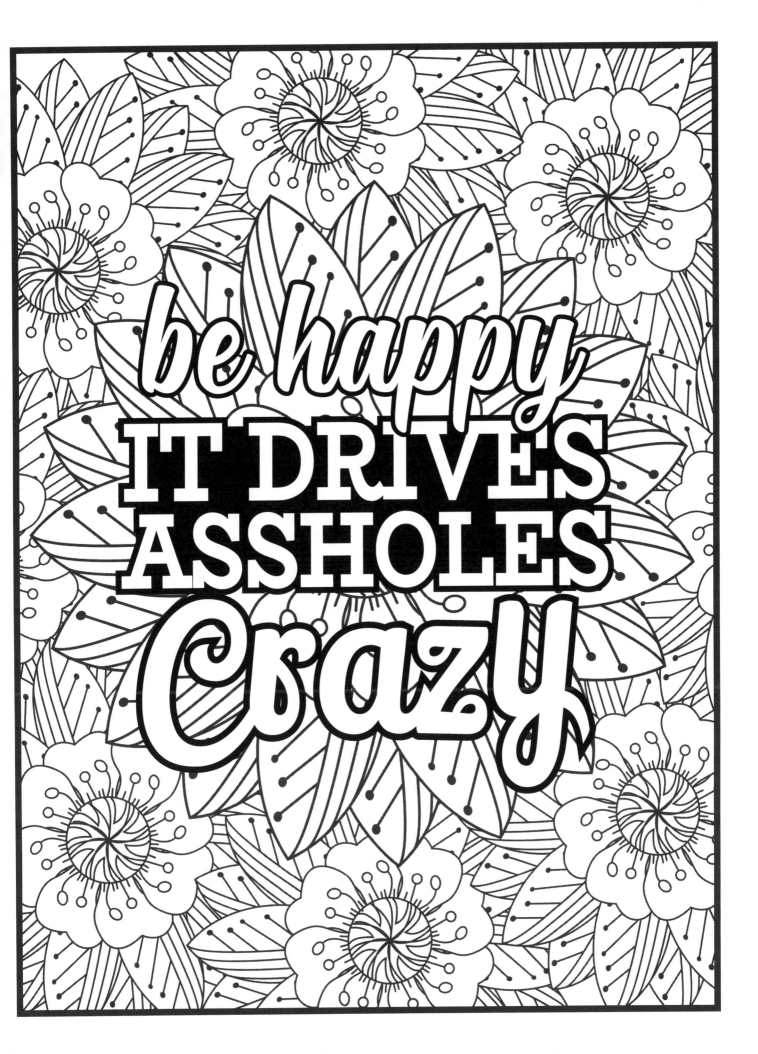

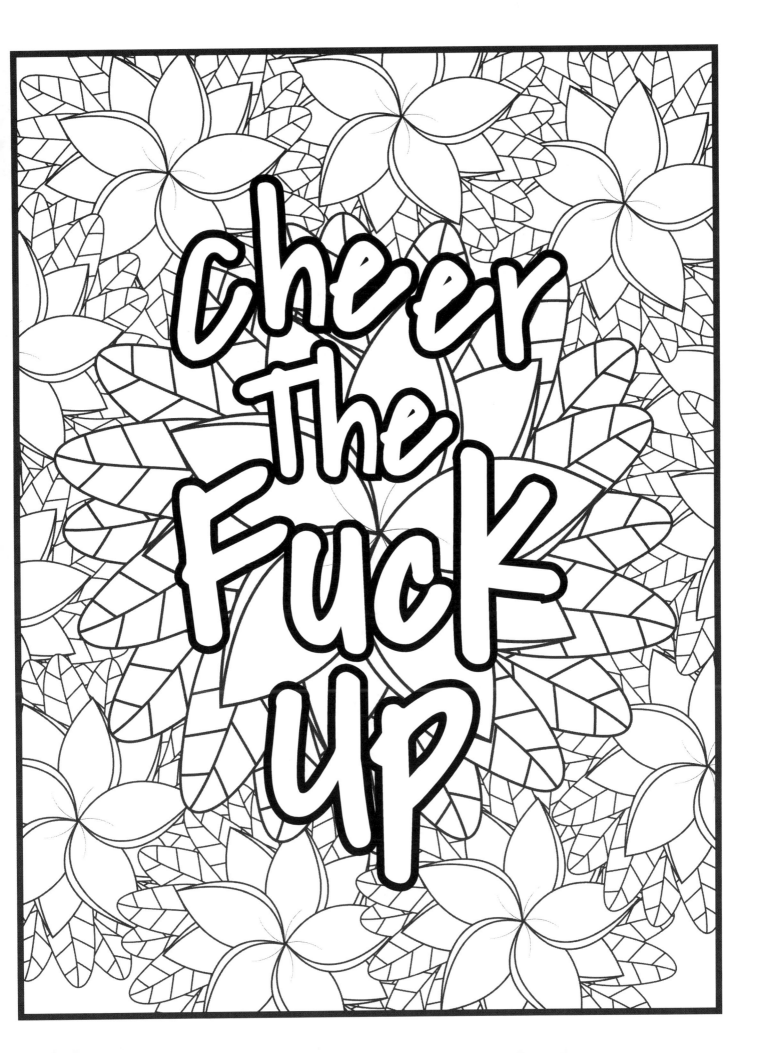

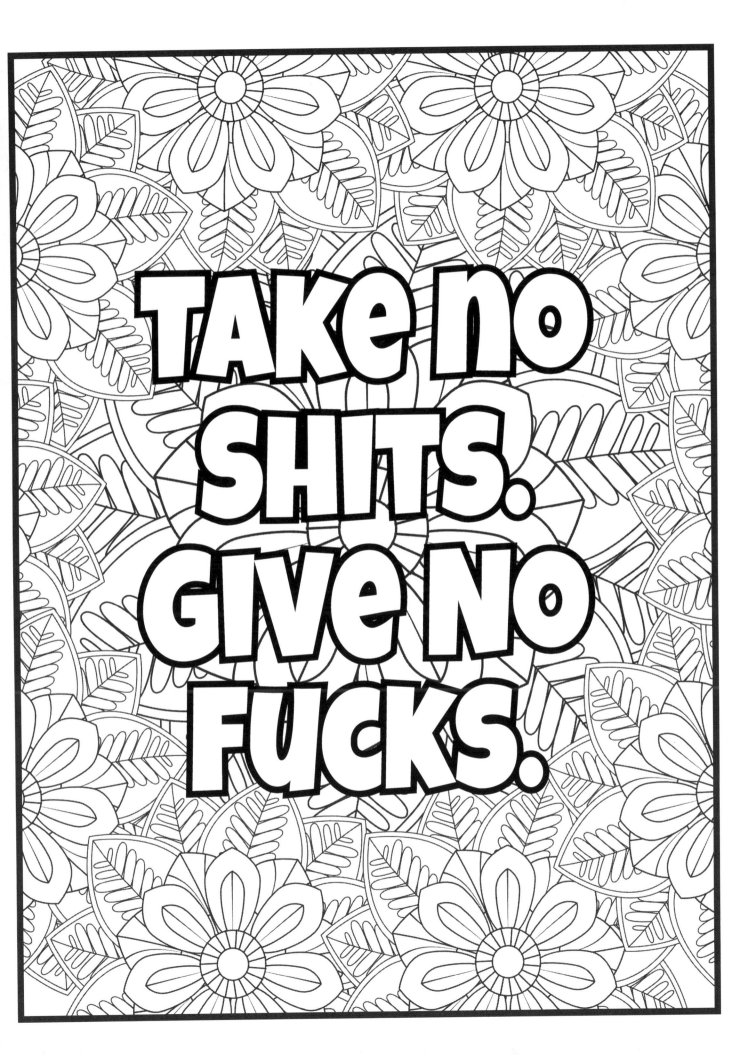

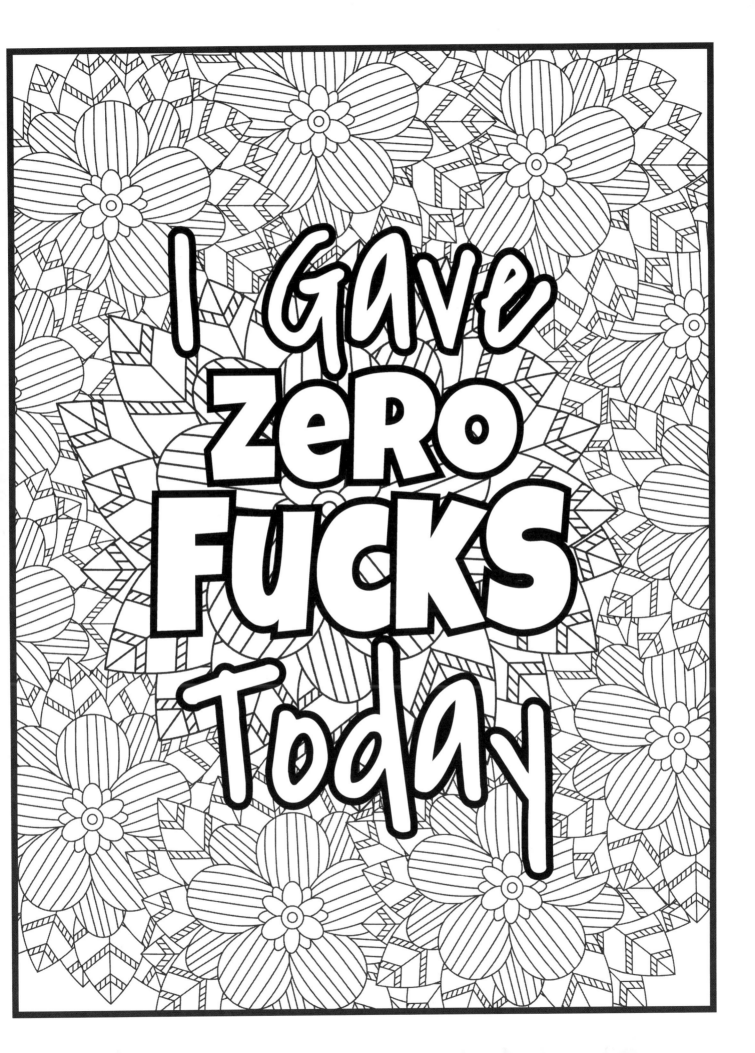

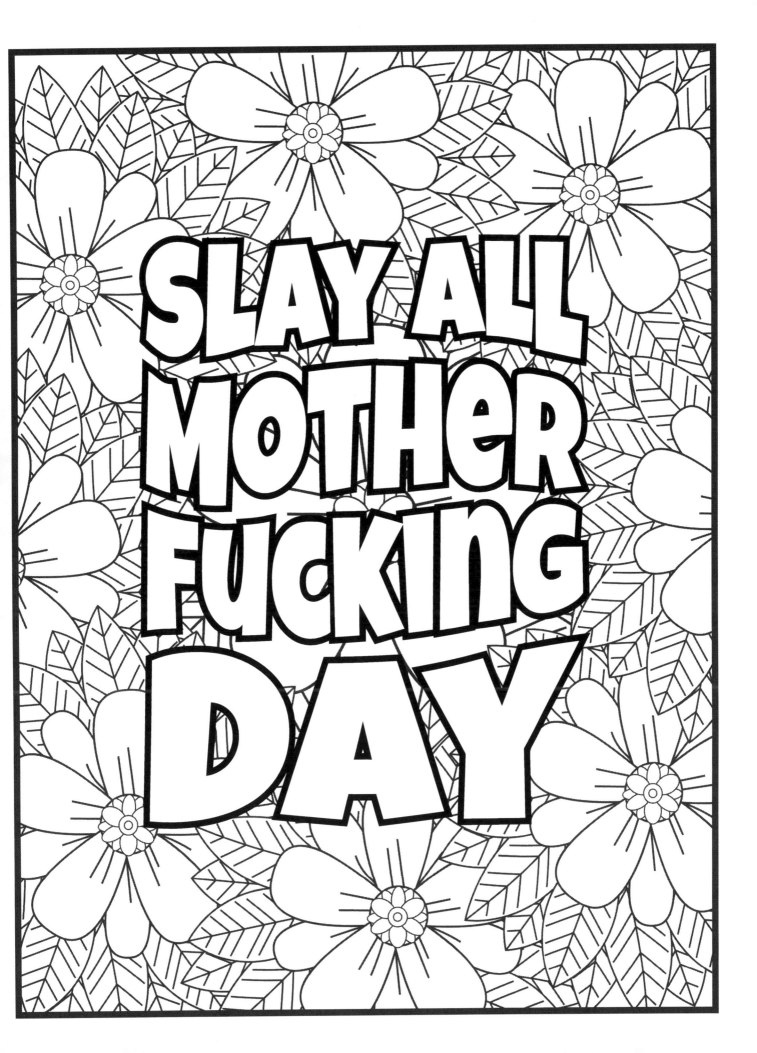

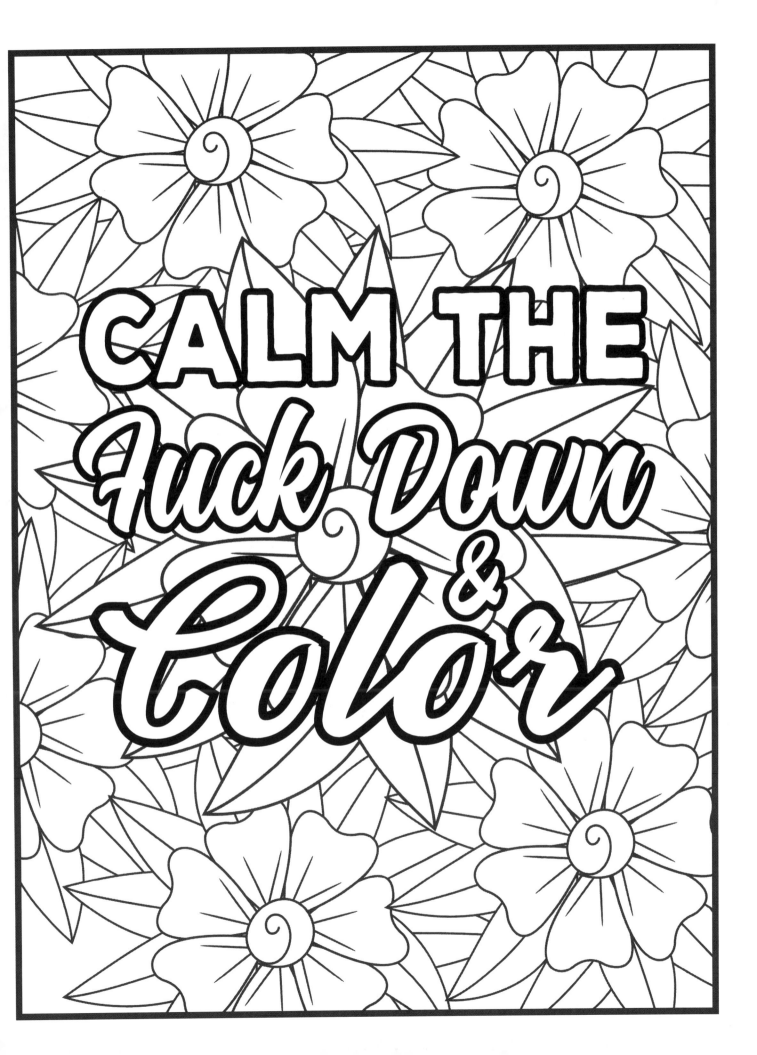

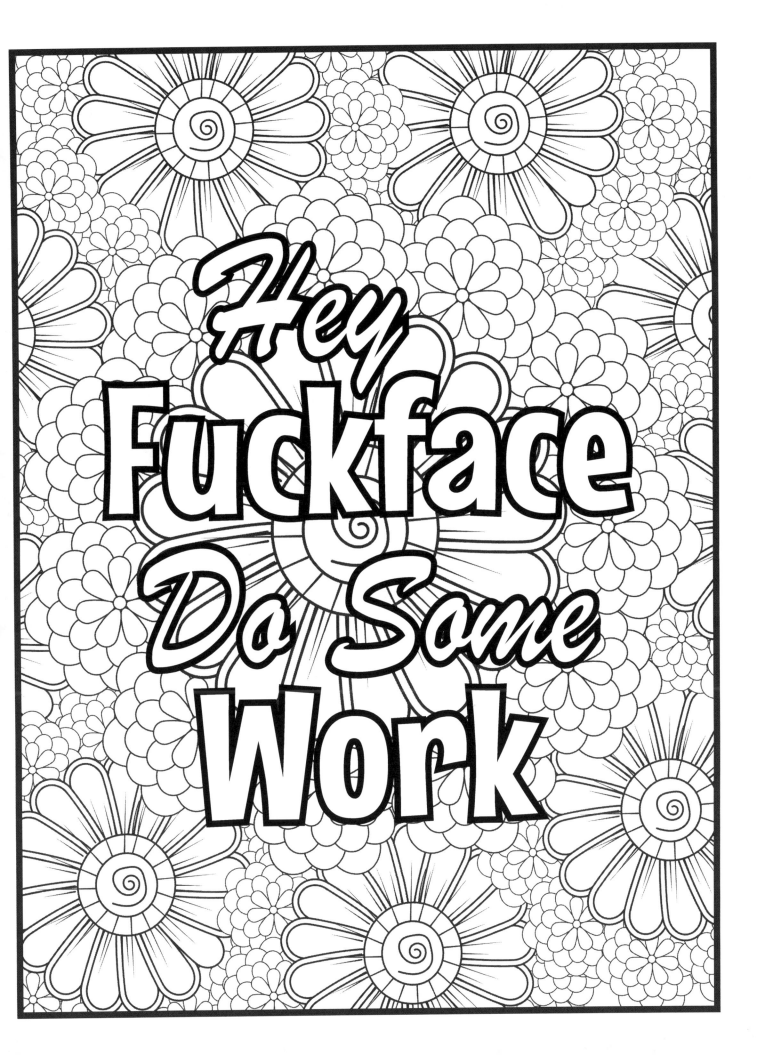

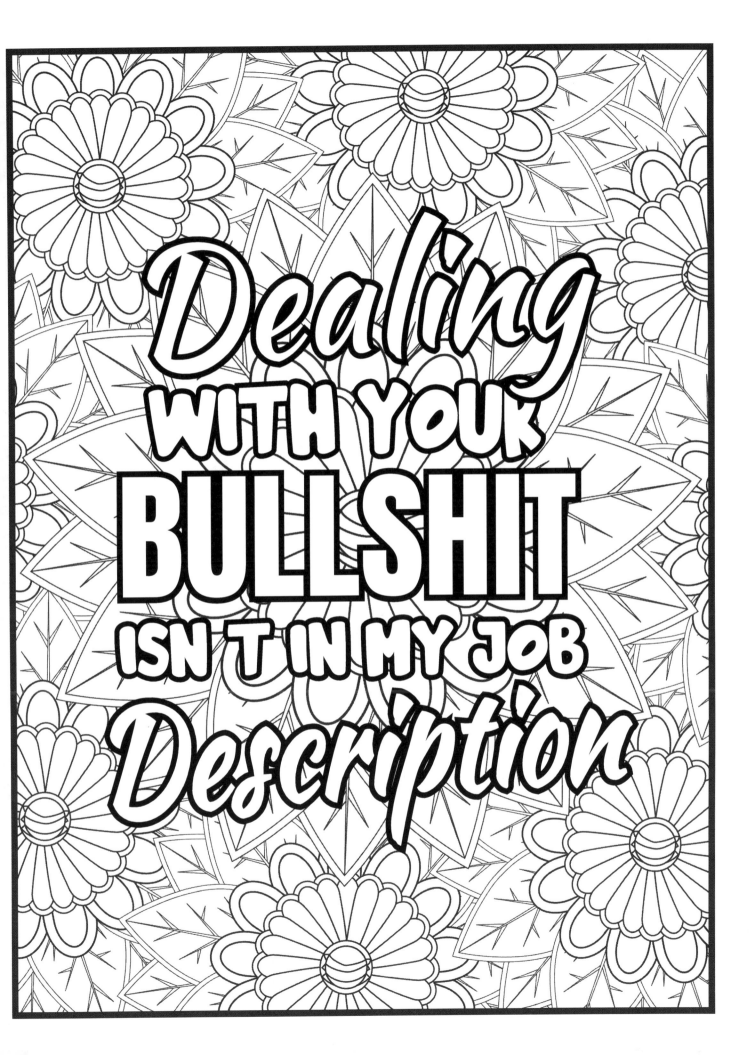

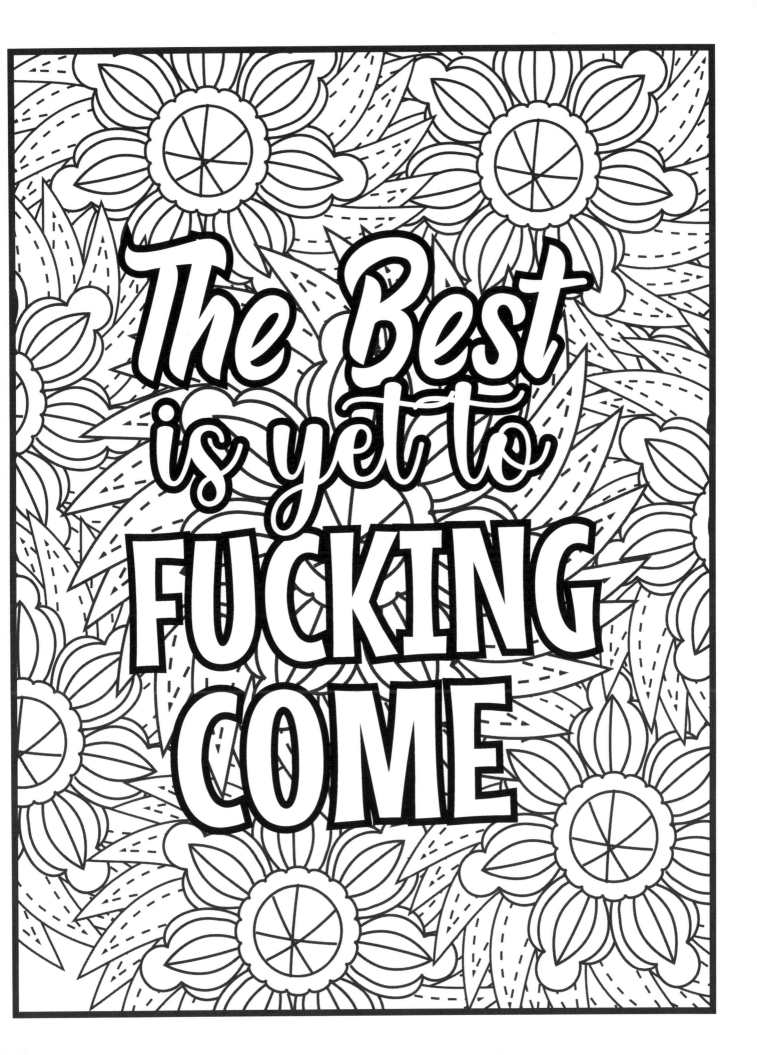

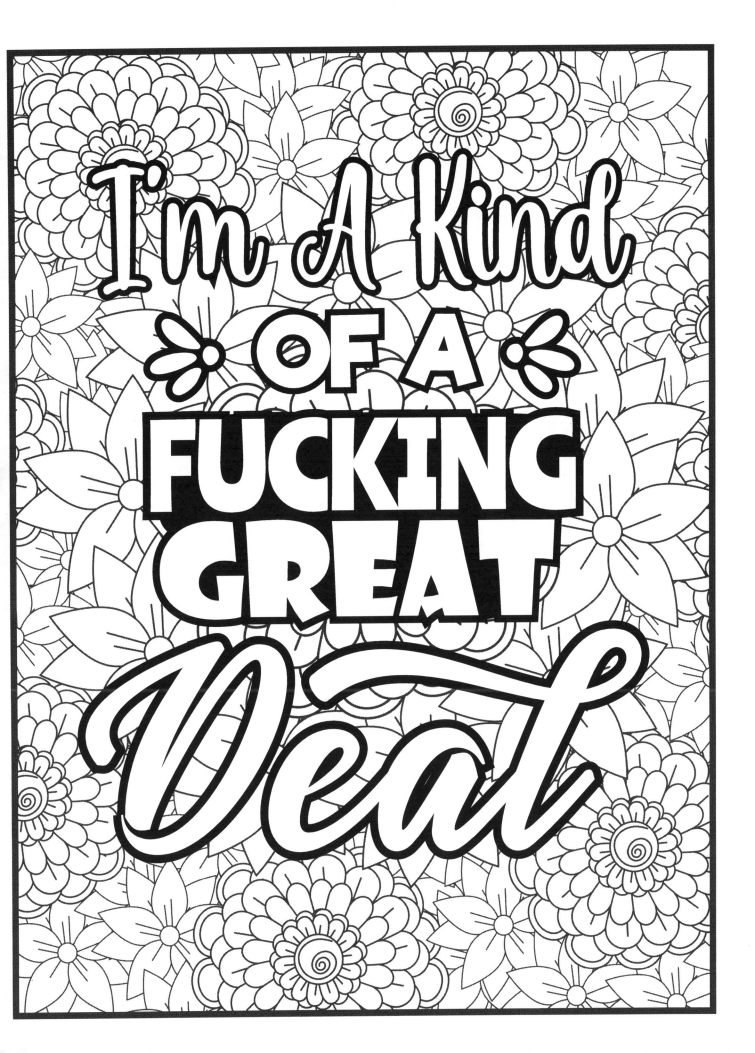

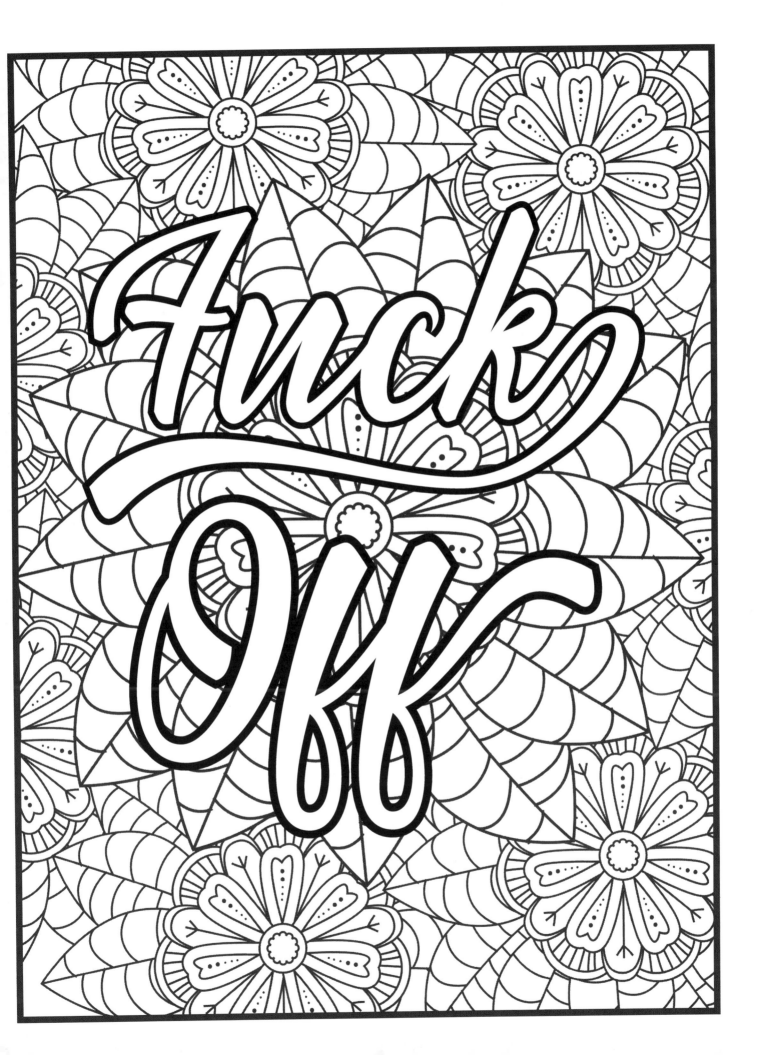

Test Your Colors

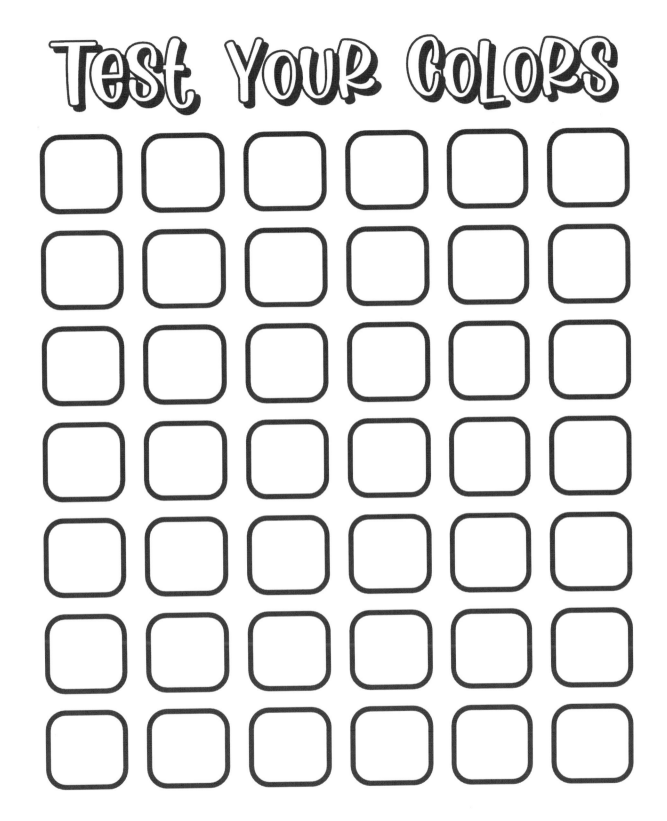

☆ ☆ ☆ ☆ ☆

Don't forget to
give us your opinion
By leaving a review

Made in the USA
Columbia, SC
07 May 2025

57633114R00046